Developing Student Discipline and Motivation

A Series for Teacher In-Service Training

Reed Martin
David Lauridsen

Research Press
2612 N. Mattis Avenue
Champaign, Illinois 61820

Contents

Introduction

Providing a humane and responsive environment for our children is the most important responsibility of our schools. But too often during the long, tedious hours of managing what seems to some teachers to be a three-ring circus, that goal is set aside. Children whom the classroom cannot tolerate are often dealt with through means such as threats, corporal punishment, the use of tranquilizing drugs, or perhaps expulsion. The use of all four is increasing at an alarming rate.

Most teachers we know want an alternative to threats, physical punishment, medication, and excluding children from school. Recent research in education, psychology and sociology have made alternatives available and a widely used method for structuring learning in a responsive environment is detailed in this book.

It is best to explore this material in a group because observations need to be shared, an understanding of the approach needs to be tested through discussion, new techniques may need to be role-played, and joint planning may need to be undertaken. Experience with this material also shows that group discussion is usually fun and rewarding.

The material, therefore, is presented in a workshop format. Ideally, each unit should be read and worked on for one week. Then the teachers should meet to exchange ideas. The task-oriented questions in each unit provide ample material for each week's discussion. By the end of Unit 7, teachers will have applied these new techniques, and Unit 8 provides a handy checklist for review.

The application of these techniques should raise questions of professional issues and ethics because lines always have to be drawn when one attempts to change another's behavior. The appendix of issue-oriented questions is included to help the workshop leader make full discussion of relevant questions a lively part of each week's meeting.

And even if after completing these units, a teacher decides not to attempt any of the structured behavior changes, he will still have gained new insight into the impact of the teacher upon developing student discipline and motivation.

Do You Have
a Behavior Problem?

If you want to influence a change in behavior, you must first observe what is sustaining the behavior at its present rate. One clue may be what happens immediately *before* the problem behavior .occurs. If you can observe and then say "Everytime *x* happens, Jimmy does *y*," then you are well on the way to understanding what stimulates that particular behavior.

However, it is more likely that what influences the behavior is what happens immediately *after* it occurs. Most behavior is learned through interaction with the social environment. If an action (whether "good" or "bad") brings a response which the actor interprets as pleasant, it is likely the action will be repeated. Since that phenomenon strengthens the behavior, it is called a *reinforcer*.

The reinforcement may be something pleasant (a child whines and whines until he gets a cookie) or the avoidance of something unpleasant (he whines until his mother says "All right, you can skip your homework tonight"). Both of these reinforce the whining behavior.

When a behavior is initially attempted, it will likely be repeated only if it is reinforced consistently by the social environment. So if a problem behavior you are concerned with is relatively new, you should be able to observe reinforcement almost every time the behavior occurs.

Once a behavior is established, however, it takes only intermittent reinforcement to maintain it. We all know from our personal experiences that we are not praised every time we do something. But an occasional positive response from our social environment brings a warm glow and keeps us going. So if the behavior you are observing is well established, you may have to watch more closely because the reinforcement will be less frequent.

In order to accurately observe a problem behavior and its reinforcement, *it is very important to deal with only one specific behavior at a time.* Obviously you cannot take Johnny's entire behavior during reading period. Take just one behavior. *It is also important that the behavior be an observable action so that we can objectively view it.* "Barbara is not interested in reading" is definitely a problem, and it may be an accurate inference, but you cannot observe what happened before or after she lost interest. "Barbara closes her book in the middle of reading and looks out the window" is an observable behavior: you can look at antecedents and consequences of that behavior. "Ann has a poor self concept" is an important problem, but where do you start? "Ann only volunteers one answer a day" gives you a place to start: what happens immediately before she volunteers and what happens immediately after? "George has a bad attitude" and it is irritating, but what behavior does George engage in that leads you to infer his attitude is bad?

The first step is to observe reinforcement theory in action. Identify a problem behavior that you feel is worth dealing with. It is probably helpful to start with just one child. Describe the behavior in specific, observable terms:

Now ask yourself two questions. First, is it a big enough problem to deal with? Suppose a child often leaves his seat to sharpen his pencil. It is against your classroom rules but does it cause enough of a problem to warrant dealing with? Second, does it happen often enough to really be a problem?

Sometimes a behavior which gets on our nerves seems to happen much more frequently than it often does. *Therefore it is important to note the frequency of the behavior.*

If the behavior you have chosen is compelling enough to be dealt with, and you have described it in specific, observable terms, then observe the behavior in action for one week. Think about what happens in the social environment preceding it and following it. Does it happen at the same time every day? Does it always involve the same children? What do you do afterwards?

As you observe, jot down any patterns that seem consistent.

Remember: do not try to change behavior this time. Just observe and analyze.

The following chart may be helpful:

PROBLEM BEHAVIOR:		
Day	How often (or how long) did it occur?	What seems to be reinforcing it?
1		
2		
3		
4		
5		

For additional reading and research documentation, see: *Modifying Classroom Behavior: A Manual of Procedure for Classroom Teachers* by Nancy K. Buckley and Hill M. Walker, pp. 3-6; *Help! These Kids Are Driving Me Crazy* by Ronald D. Carter, pp. 13-16; *New Tools for Changing Behavior* by Alvin N. Deibert and Alice J. Harmon, pp. 1-16. Published by Research Press, 2612 N. Mattis, Champaign, Illinois 61820.

2

Observing Your Own Behavior

You are the most important part of your students' school environment. Your reaction to what they do influences each child's social and academic behavior.

In the last unit you got some practice describing and observing another's behavior. It is vital that you also be aware of your own behavior. You are in a constant social exchange with your students: while you reinforce them, they also reinforce you. This process is inevitable and occurs whether we wish it or not. So it is important for you to observe your own behavior—to look over your own shoulder—to see what you are being reinforced for doing. This is important because if you wish to change the behavior of one of your students, you might have to change your own behavior. To change your own behavior, you must first observe it in action.

An equally important reason to observe your own behavior is that you also influence the behavior of others through the principle of *modeling*. Most of us have significant other persons in our lives whom we attempt to imitate. We may perform an act because we have seen them perform it and it seems to pay off for them. Or we may do it just for the joy of seeming to be like the model we are imitating—in speech, dress, or other behavior. You have undoubtedly seen some of your students imitating you—for better or worse.

Your behavior is important, so you should practice looking at it.

HOW POSITIVE ARE YOU?

How much positive feedback do you give to others in your social environment? In a one-hour period, mark down the number of times that you react pleasantly (smile, praise, etc.) to someone else's behavior. We're not advocating insincerity: that will show through and your praise will lose its potency. What we want is for you to find as many praiseworthy behaviors as possible and respond to them in a positive way that is observable to the other person.

The following chart may be helpful. And you may want to try the exercise several times—both to practice finding more praiseworthy behaviors and to practice reacting positively.

ONE HOUR OF POSITIVE REINFORCEMENT	
Your behavior	**How many times?**
Smile, nod head Praise, attention Other _____	_____ _____ _____ _____ _____

WHAT REINFORCES YOU?

As you interact with students or others at school, note five things that others do in response to you that give you a warm glow. (You might want to adopt the same reinforcing behaviors and use them yourself.)

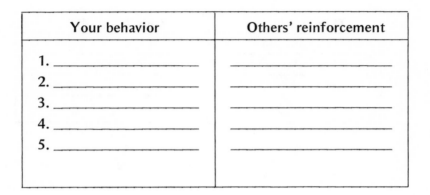

Your behavior	Others' reinforcement
1. _____	_____
2. _____	_____
3. _____	_____
4. _____	_____
5. _____	_____

WHAT TURNS YOU OFF?

As you interact with students and others, note three things that others do that make it less likely that you will engage in that specific interaction again. It may be an unpleasant response or no response at all. (You might want to make sure that you do not unintentionally do those unpleasant things.)

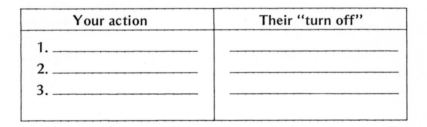

Your action	Their "turn off"
1. _____	_____
2. _____	_____
3. _____	_____

HOW DO YOU TURN OTHERS OFF?

In interactions with students and others, note three things that you do to indicate you would like them not to engage in that behavior again. (Are these successful in turning off their behavior or do they merely make you unpleasant?)

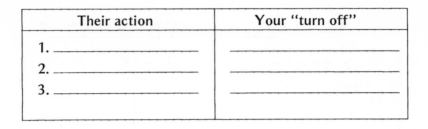

Their action	Your "turn off"
1. _____	_____
2. _____	_____
3. _____	_____

WHAT MAKES YOU "LOSE CONTROL"?

No one has to tell you teaching can be frustrating. Physical wear by the end of each day may add to your emotional drain. When you are really "down," possibly near the end of the day, another's action might provoke in you a reaction much stronger than otherwise. This might be when a particularly disruptive child tries to make you lose your cool, and thus abandon your plan for changing his behavior. As you learn to observe your own behavior, you can detect cues that let you know your social balance is being upset. If you catch them in time, you can stay in control of your own behavior—which is your goal if you are to try to change another's behavior.

Note five things that make you tense up or overreact. Think of ways to relax or act cool.

Provocative event	Cue that you are getting tense	What alternative?
1. _____	_____	_____
2. _____	_____	_____
3. _____	_____	_____
4. _____	_____	_____
5. _____	_____	_____

DO YOU NEED
A MORE REINFORCING ENVIRONMENT?

When we feel "depressed" we often are running short on reinforcement. What are you doing at school that you feel deserves reinforcement and is not being recognized?

What are others doing that you might reinforce?

3

Analyzing the Classroom Environment

The socially disruptive behavior that often requires discipline may occur in conjunction with academic failure or lack of motivation. Much educational research in the past few years has centered on the problem of what causes failure. Some children who otherwise seem capable of performing satisfactorily seem not to even want to try. They seem to prefer causing disruption. Could they have "learned" to behave this way?

We have been examining rules by which all of us learn behavior and they apply to students' academic as well as social behavior. We have examined the teacher as the most important part of the environment in the classroom but now it is time to look at the presentation of curriculum and other things in the classroom environment which help students learn whether trying will pay off.

We all learn in a social context and use what we've learned in the past to predict the future. When we approach what might seem like a new situation, we draw on pieces of our past experiences which seem similar. And we use what we learned in those past experiences to guide our conduct—to choose things that we predict will succeed in producing a positive result and to avoid things that we predict will fail to produce anything good.

We can call these bits of our learned history *cues.*

Suppose you are a dynamite charades player but cannot tolerate bridge. One evening some friends suggest playing a game. You suggest playing charades and immediately you are turned on as your mind cues pleasant things that you have learned to associate with your success at charades. Someone else suggests the group play bridge, the majority agrees, and you immediately start having a bad time. Nothing has happened yet—the situation has simply cued a past failure and you see nothing hopeful in continuing. You won't even try.

Cues are also important in academic performance. When a student is confronted with a curricular task, the *conditions* under which it is presented, and the *consequences* of attempting the task, may cue a response. If a student has no chance of success at the task you have assigned him, he will probably perform another behavior (daydream, act sick, disrupt the classroom, claim he did not understand the directions, leave his book and assignment at home) rather than engage in a predictable failure. The other behaviors mentioned above may bring a predictable success. The student has probably done them in the past and either gotten a pleasant response such as your attention or his peers' laughter, or he has removed, or temporarily avoided, something unpleasant such as the assignment.

One alternative is to make sure the student can experience success at the task assigned and thus develop a pleasant association which will make trying again in the future more likely. This does not mean that the material should not challenge the student. And it certainly does not mean we "lower our standards" and give any kind of work an "A." What it does mean is that we have to structure the presentation of curricular materials to make success probable.

To see how easily conditions and consequences can get in the way of success, let's imagine how we would set things up if we wanted to guarantee that children would lose interest in the curriculum and begin to disrupt the class and eventually give up on school.

CONDITIONS THAT CUE POOR RESPONSES

First, to guarantee failure, pick a subject matter area where the student has failed in the past. That means when you say, "Let's work on x" the student will see no chance for anything positive to happen. He has always failed in the past and he is likely to think you are almost taunting him by saying "Try one more time." (As an extreme example of this, an inmate at Lorton Reformatory near Washington, D.C. once observed that the mandatory education classes were the worst part of his punishment because they were so humiliating.)

Second, to assure failure, make sure the assignment is written on a reading level too advanced for the student. A student who can barely read during reading class cannot become a fast reader simply because the class is now on social studies. This includes reading test questions. If you pass out a mathematics exercise which reads "Compute the sum of two and two," are you testing mathematics ability or tripping up a poor reader?

Third, if you still want to guarantee failure, make sure the assignment is vague. Since we respond to predictable situations, a vague assignment may be left undone. Why take a chance and read the wrong 10 pages, or do the wrong 10 problems, and then find out, probably in front of the whole class, that you have goofed again. It is more likely the student will leave it undone and seek an activity with a predictably positive return.

Fourth, make the tasks too difficult. If a student is having trouble with simple addition, move the whole class ahead to fractions and leave him falling farther and farther behind.

Fifth, make sure the material is boring. If the student responds well to programmed material done on his own, then present the material in a lecture format. And make the content boring. If a twelve-year-old reads only at the third grade level and the only material at that level is about Peter Rabbit, fine.

Sixth, make sure there is not enough time, either to complete the assignment satisfactorily or to develop an interest in it.

These six conditions will probably cue a poor response to the curricular task. But, even if these conditions were corrected and the student attempts to perform the task, the consequences of that attempt might cue poor behavior in the future.

CONSEQUENCES THAT CUE POOR RESPONSES

The following five situations show how easily you could intentionally cause consequences that would cue poor responses.

First, grade the work on a group basis so that the students on the bottom will most likely stay on the bottom.

Second, make the consequence of successfully performing the task something which you think is nice (a gold star?) but which is virtually neutral to the student.

Third, reward only a complete assignment, even if the student was trying very hard.

Fourth, once the student has turned in an assignment, give a final grade. Do not let the student see his mistakes, then try the assignment over and let him have an opportunity to improve his grades.

Fifth, concentrate more of your attention on the student's failure and non-performance than you do on trying or even the successful completion of a task.

ANALYZING THE CLASSROOM ENVIRONMENT

As you present your next lesson or assignment in an area in which a particular student has had trouble, note the following:

1. Is the subject area one in which the student has always failed?

2. Can the student read at whatever level the material is presented?

3. Is the assignment clear enough so the student knows exactly what is expected?

4. Is the task at a level of difficulty that is challenging but which offers a chance of successful completion for that individual (rather than for the class average)?

5. Is the material presented in a manner which seems to interest the student: written, lecture, audio-visual, programmed workbook, independent work, group assignments, etc.? And is the material content of interest?

6. Is enough time allowed to get into the assignment and develop an interest, and to complete it satisfactorily?

7. Will the student be graded on an individual basis so that successful completion will get a good grade?

8. Is there a pleasant consequence that you know appeals to the student (possibly chosen by the student) that will follow successful completion of the task?

9. Is there some motivating consequence to at least complete part of the assignment, even if the student cannot complete all of it?

10. Do you give the student another chance to do the assignment correctly and to improve the grade?

11. Do you give more attention to the student when he tries a task than you do when he refuses to try?

Your analysis of the conditions under which tasks are presented to students, and the consequences of students attempting those tasks, may point up problems which are motivation problems, but which may also be sources of some of your worst discipline problems.

For additional analysis along this line, see: *Developing Attitude Toward Learning* by Robert F. Mager, especially pp. 39-48. Published by Fearon Publishers, 6 Davis Drive, Belmont, California 94002.

Basic Principles
of Human Behavior

4

Much recent research in the science of human relationships suggests that behaviors are made up of many little pieces that have been learned in a social environment. If children learn behavior, it follows that *teachers teach behavior*.

The first step in understanding how behavior can be taught, and how it can be changed, is to observe it. You have now had practice at observing some basic human interactions: on the part of your students (Unit 1), how you interact with your own environment (Unit 2), and the influence of how curriculum is presented (Unit 3).

The next task is to learn how to change a specific behavior in a way that will facilitate learning. We must begin by elaborating on the basic principles of behavior that you have been observing so that you can draw on them in future units.

1.   **A behavior is some specific human activity that we can all see and can all agree occurred.** For example, "Johnny loves school" is not a behavior, it is an inference; "Johnny comes early, stays late and asks for extra assignments" is a behavior.

It is useful to talk in terms of observable "behaviors" for several reasons. First, it allows us to describe acts without labeling the actor. If we are faced with a student who is physically aggressive, then we can focus on that act. But if we label the student "disturbed," we are less able to work on the specific problem and we may, in fact, create a bigger one. Labels often turn into self-fulfilling prophecies and send children down dead-end bureaucratic streets.

A second reason to deal with observable behaviors is that everyone concerned can agree that the problem behavior exists. One teacher may feel Johnny needs help because of a "poor self concept" while another feels his "self concept" is fine. If they were to work on the specific observable behaviors from which they infer their judgment about "self concept," then Johnny might get the help he needs.

Third, with observable behaviors everyone can see the effect of their intervention: they can tell whether they are helping or hurting. Fourth, we can clarify our expectations more easily as we deal with students. Saying, "Don't get into trouble" or "I want you to make me proud of you" can leave a student not sure what he is supposed to do and what he is not supposed to do. Being specific about what social behavior is desired is as necessary as specificity about academic assignments.

Fifth, if we focus on behavior it is much more likely that we can communicate our feelings without losing tempers or hurting relationships. A teacher can indicate that a particular action is not desirable without indicating that the child is not liked. This permits the teacher to act more dispassionately and avoid making value-laden judgmental statements which seem to provoke students so readily.

2. **The probability that a behavior will be repeated is strongly influenced by what happens immediately after it occurs.** This is only common sense—we all learn through experience. A pleasant result will strengthen (reinforce) the likelihood that the behavior engaged in will be repeated.

3. **Reinforcement should follow the behavior as quickly as possible.** Imagine the impact on a student who turns in a good assignment and is told "good job" versus waiting two weeks to get any reaction.

4. **Reinforcement should be of value to the person receiving it.** This may be the crux of many failures in human interaction. First, we often feel that good activity has value in itself so we assume it is self-rewarding and we offer no positive response of our own. We do not tell someone he did a good job; we just assume that he will be proud of himself. But we then run the risk that the individual is not actually self-rewarded and since the action received no positive response from us, it may be weakened or discontinued. Second, if we do offer a rewarding response, it is often something that has value to us or which we think ought to be rewarding to the other person (for example, a trip to a museum or a gold star). If that works—that is, if the behavior is strengthened and occurs again and again—then fine. But if it does not work, remember the principle: a behavior that you want to be repeated must receive immediate reinforcement which is valued by the recipient.

5. **There are different types of reinforcement: intrinsic reinforcement and extrinsic reinforcement.** Intrinsic reinforcement is the pleasure or satisfaction we experience when we have performed well on a task or activity— the reward is in the doing. This is a basic ingredient in self-control and self-motivation.

   Research suggests that when a person is intinsically reinforced for something, he probably received extrinsic reinforcement in the beginning. Then as successful performance of the action became rewarding in itself, the extrinsic motivation was less important and intrinsic values took over. A typical example is speech. In the beginning we get much praise for our efforts, but eventually speech is engaged in because it has very natural intrinsic rewards.

Some tasks, particularly those at which we fail, bring no intrinsic reward. In those cases an extrinsic reinforcement may be needed to get the person to engage in the behavior and to make it "rewarding." Although we may all earnestly desire it, many students are not imbued with the "pure joy of learning."

Extrinsic reinforcements fall into several types. The strongest and most abundant is *social reinforcement*—attention, praise. Another type is *privileges and special activities*—getting to engage in some activity you desire. A third type is *material objects*—some material item like a game, or a consumable item like crayons and a coloring book. A fourth type is *tokens*—points, gold stars, or checkmarks that can be accumulated and turned in for privileges and special activities or material objects. Two additional types are *grades and commendations* and *edibles.*

Each of these types of reinforcement already exists in the everyday world. We are all constantly giving and taking social reinforcement. We work toward preferred activities. All of us use material objects, and most of us work for tokens, like money, which we can exchange for another type of reinforcement.

The influence of our social environment on each of us varies just as human beings vary. Some people more quickly respond to social reinforcement, while others will strive more for material rewards. Some people seem only to do something if it has a "pay-off" but luckily others will do things apparently just because it makes them feel good about themselves.

We are not advocating the use of extrinsic rewards if intrinsic reinforcement is already present. But research shows one can encourage an activity with extrinsic reinforcement and then fade the extrinsic feature until it is no longer needed. The reason is that if the extrinsic reward will get the person to engage in the behavior, and if it is structured so the initial experiences can be successful, then the reward of successful performance will probably keep it going.

6. **In the real world, reinforcement doesn't always immediately follow performance, nor does it occur after every performance; reinforcement is often intermittent and delayed.** We do not have to get trapped into rewarding everything a child does—we can systematically *fade* out through intermittent reinforcement. (Specific techniques will be discussed in a later unit.) And, the child will not become dependent upon immediate rewards, but can actually be taught to delay gratification—one of the basic elements of self-control and growth. Equally important, individuals must learn to take the future into account by realizing that some acts bring immediate pleasure but over the long run may bring pain.

7. **Behavior is also influenced by negative reinforcement, the removal of something unpleasant.** Negative reinforcement shouldn't be confused with punishment simply because of the term "negative." It is "negative" because the consequence is *removed or avoided*; "reinforcement" because the likelihood for repetition of the behavior is strengthened. If a child cries, you pick her up and she stops, you have been negatively reinforced. Something unpleasant to you (crying) stopped after your action (picking the child up). If a boy whines for a cookie after you have said "No more cookies" and you give him one, you have been negatively reinforced (something unpleasant stopped) and the boy has been positively reinforced (he got something pleasant). Since both actions were reinforced (strengthened) it is likely they will be repeated. If a class is noisy and the teacher yells "Shut up" and it works, the teacher is likely to do it again. The key to using this principle is to learn how to remove unpleasant things from our environment without becoming unpleasant ourselves.

Negative reinforcement is very strong and it may lead to bad behavior. If a child involved in a fight can escape unpleasant consequences by lying, then the principle of negative reinforcement may lead him to lie. We have all seen this in young children who begin to tell stories about why they could not do their homework or about how something got broken. The best approach is to make the (positive) reinforcement for performance more attractive than the (negative) reinforcement for escaping the penalty for non-performance.

8. **Punishment also exists in the real world. It is any feedback from the environment which decreases the future performance of a behavior.** This means you have to look at the consequences of your interaction, not just your intention. If you intend to punish, but the result is that a child continues to engage in a particular action, then you are not punishing, and in fact you may be reinforcing.

One problem all of us have in our interpersonal relations is that we sometimes unintentionally punish good behavior or unintentionally reward bad behavior. Remember: these rules all apply to good and bad behavior alike. We can teach bad behavior as easily as good behavior if we are not careful to observe the consequences of our social interactions and make sure that bad behavior does not pay off.

Punishment (weakening a behavior) is the opposite of reinforcement (strengthening a behavior) and involves opposite techniques: structuring an unpleasant consequence after a behavior or removing a pleasant consequence. But punishment should be used sparingly because it creates problems. Effective punishment should terminate a behavior, but often what happens is that we simply suppress the behavior and when the punishment is removed the behavior starts again. This can lead to a larger dose of punishment, then a larger one—and where do you stop? Substitute teachers often face this problem. Punishment can occur in the form of threats ("Do that once more and I'll have you suspended from school") which are ignored because the child knows the adult is not likely to follow through.

A second problem is that pure punishment teaches no behavior. If two children are punished for fighting, they have still not learned how to play together. A third, related problem is that children learn how to avoid punishment: lying, cheating, truancy, feigning illness and so forth. So your attempt at punishment may not only not teach a positive behavior but, in fact, may teach an undesired behavior.

Fourth, administering punishment may make a person very unpleasant to a child. If the child consequently begins to avoid that person, then there is less chance to be a positive influence. Similarly, we have observed how a word of praise can be very reinforcing at times. But if a person becomes unpleasant, then "praise" from him may lose its potency. This does not mean one must never punish, or must never exercise authority and say "No." But it does suggest that we must provide unpleasant consequences, when they are warranted, without being unpleasant ourselves.

A fifth problem with punishment occurs when a physically superior person punishes another through some physical means. The lesson that might be taught, unintentionally, is "When you are big enough you can make others do things." Studies of children who are physically aggressive show they have often been subjected to a lot of physical punishment. We must be careful not to teach aggressiveness when we think we are simply punishing bad behavior.

A final problem is that punishment forces us to focus on undesired behavior and perhaps distracts us from seeing good behavior. Assume we want a child to work on an assignment rather than repeatedly disturbing another child. If we use punishment, we must focus attention on the disruption and we may miss opportunities to respond positively to any good features in the behavior.

9.   **Another thing happens in the real world which decreases behavior and that is a neutral response.** If we do something and get no reaction time after time, then it is less likely we will put any effort into doing that in the future. This can be a very good tool if we use it intentionally, but if we do not know what we are doing, and simply ignore some child's consistent performance of some task, that child may eventually stop performing. Positive feedback is so important that its absence—a neutral response— may terminate a behavior.

Observing and understanding behavior is the key to changing it. For review of these basic principles, see if you can observe the following either at school or at home.

TYPES OF REINFORCEMENT

1. Acts which appear to be *intrinsically* reinforced (positively):

2. Acts which are *extrinsically* reinforced (positively):

3. Acts which are *negatively* reinforced:

4. Acts which are not reinforced at all:

5. Acts which are *continuously* reinforced:

6. Acts which are *intermittently* reinforced:

7. Some common social reinforcers:

8. Some common activity reinforcers:

9. Some common material reinforcers:

10. Some common token reinforcers:

PROBLEMS WITH PUNISHMENT

1. Intended punishment which was unintentionally rewarding:

2. Intended reinforcement which unintentionally punished:

3. Examples of ineffective punishment that lead to even larger doses of punishment:

4. Threats that cannot be carried out:

5. Avoidance behaviors which a child uses to escape punishment:

6. Persons becoming "unpleasant" to children because of being punishing:

7. Examples of punishment that teach aggressive behavior:

8. Examples of dwelling on undesired aspects of behavior and missing opportunities to praise:

Planning for Change

5

Researchers and others who attempt to systematically influence behavior have found it useful to employ the following plan. There are three main phases: an *analysis* of the situation, a strategy for *change* if any is desired, and an *evaluation* of what worked and what else is needed.

I. ANALYSIS

A. Identify the "Problem" in Terms of an Observable Behavior

The problem is probably the gap between what you expect a student to be doing in a particular case, and what his actual performance is. This means that in regard to your expectation, you must have a definite observable objective in mind. "Johnny does not do well in math" does not give us much information. "Johnny had an assignment to work for 5 minutes on math and he got up and started wandering around after 2 minutes" tells us what the expected performance was.

And you must specify what the actual performance was, and not bury it under a descriptive label. "Johnny never finishes his 5-minute math assignments because he is hyperactive" does not give enough information.

In order to get this information, for academic or social behavior, you must have a clear expectation and objective, not subjective, information on performance.

Now that we have a describable gap—a problem—there are three alternatives. *The first is to consider tolerating it.* How important a problem is it? A few years ago many students were expelled for violating dress codes—girls with slacks, boys with long hair. They all had a gap between what their teachers and principals felt was expected behavior and actual behavior. But was it really that important?

A better way to address this aspect of the problem is to ask "What would happen if you left it alone?" If you have a student who is falling farther and farther behind, you obviously should not label him "slow" or "unmotivated" and fail to attempt to remove the gap. You must decide when the problem is worth solving.

The second alternative is to reduce the gap between expectation and performance by lowering your expectation. This is often done unintentionally: a teacher's expectation for a child is lessened day after day until little is expected and little is received. We have all read of research into self-fulfilling prophecies in which a teacher is told a student has a low I.Q., lowers her expectations, and the student performs poorly.

So we should be careful to maintain high enough expectations for each child to challenge him, but not so high as to defeat him. Taking into account all the conditions surrounding the assigned task, ask "Can the expectation be met?" A student who reads poorly, has failed in math, and does poorly on written work, if asked to work quietly on math for 30 minutes, may find it impossible to do. A student who never sat still for 5 minutes in the second grade cannot be expected to start the third grade and sit still for hours. That is one of the features that makes teachers so important in the development of their students: you must choose tasks that are developmentally possible, that are not so easy they are boring or so difficult they are defeating; and you must see that a child receives special outside help when it is needed, but be careful not to label a child a "special" case.

Assuming we have a gap, that it is too much of a problem to be tolerated, and that your expectation is achievable by the student—*the third alternative is to remove the gap by increasing performance.*

B. Observe the Performance Deficits in Action and Indicate the Circumstances

When does it occur? Where does it occur? Is it related to a particular subject matter or a particular person? Are there obstacles to successful performance? Some students perform well, but on the wrong assignment. Is it perfectly clear what you expect the student to do, and when? Are there other obstacles: an insufficient amount of time, a virtual inability to read, or a temporary health problem? How frequently does the performance gap occur? If the behavior is quite frequent (for example, leaving one's seat and wandering around several times an hour), then you might want to graph it so you can measure your progress. The following type of graph is often used for this purpose.

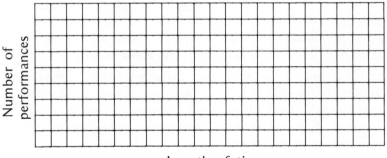

Graphing is very helpful for another reason. If you focus attention well enough to count the occurrences, you will find you are observing well. Or an alternative is to have a third party (such as a counselor or administrator) sit in the class and count behaviors (assuming his presence will not substantially change behavior).

C. Analyze the Behavior

You should now know the *conditions* under which the behavior arises: when, where, how often, in relation to what subject matter or what persons, and whether there are obstacles like unclear instructional objectives. We might be able to analyze something that explains the behavior.

But most likely we will have to examine the *consequences* of performance (or non-performance) to analyze the behavior.

First, is there any positive consequence to performance? As we have explored in earlier units, if performance has no consequence of value to the recipient, then the student may cease to perform your task and do something else which brings a consequence more immediate or more pleasant.

The most common problem occurs when a student simply gets no feedback whatsoever. Think of how many activities we are asked to engage in that bring no consequence except escaping a penalty for non-performance. The development of the "teaching machine," programmed instruction and individualized instruction followed the realization that frequent feedback (even if it is "You picked the wrong answer, try again") is better than no consequence.

Second, is performance of some other behavior rewarding? If a student can get the *same* reward by some other means, such as cheating on homework or a test, then he may try that. If the student can get a *different* reward by another means, but he values that reward equally or greater than the one offered by your task, then that may influence his behavior. For example, if daydreaming or disrupting the class brings a consequence more pleasant than that following the performance of your task, you may see daydreaming and disruption.

Third, is the performance you desire likely to bring a punishing consequence? For example, you may ask the writer of the best report to read it to the class. If a student is shy, your consequence might be punishing.

Remember, we are concerned with gaps between what you realistically expect in both academic and social behavior and what is actually performed. Some students will not need an immediate consequence; some will prefer completing an assignment to cheating; some will be stimulated by your asking them to read their papers to the class. But if a student seems poorly motivated, then analyze his behavior by asking the following questions: Is there any consequence? Is there an equal consequence for performing a different behavior? Is the performance followed by any punishing consequences?

II. CHANGE STRATEGY

You have now selected a problem, observed it, and analyzed the conditions under which it occurs and the consequences that follow either performance or non-performance. That analysis is needed to select a strategy for change.

A. Choose a Goal

First, determine whether the change involves increasing or decreasing a behavior, or both. That will influence your choice of change strategies.

Second, discuss the goal with all others who you feel must be involved, for example, the student himself, other teachers, other students, members of the family. Obviously the depth of explanation will differ depending upon the person's age, degree of involvement and so forth.

B. Plan Your Strategy

The specifics of your strategy will be discussed in the remaining units. To apply them you must note what is maintaining the behavior at its current unsatisfactory level, and you must select alternative rewarding consequences which you are willing to use and which will be motivating to the student involved. You should not ignore the rewards and punishments that already occur and simply add others on top of them.

And to the greatest extent possible, involve the student and others in the choice of a strategy and in its implementation.

III. EVALUATION

A crucial point in any evaluation is the decision as to what to use as a measure. By dealing with a specific problem behavior, setting a specific goal, and observing specific performance, you prevent many measurement problems.

One common mistake, however, is to use a measure that catches only large changes. This means you must wait too long or for too great a change in performance to notice a difference. And if that means you must delay rewards until a significant change occurs, then the first few steps in the right direction may get no reinforcement and change may be thwarted. So, be sure you can measure interim progress—changes short of the final goal.

A final evaluation problem involves *maintenance*. Once you successfully change a behavior to a level that you feel is good, then a different strategy will be needed to maintain that level. Obviously you will not at that point continue a rigorous daily evaluation schedule, but you will want to have a way to check back occasionally and make sure things are still satisfactory—that your behavior change strategy was a success.

For additional information on these topics and research documentation, see: *New Tools for Changing Behavior* by Alvin N. Deibert and Alice J. Harmon, pp. 37-53; *Help, These Kids Are Driving Me Crazy* by

Ronald D. Carter, pp. 63-84; *Modifying Classroom Behavior: A Manual of Procedure for Classroom Teachers* by Nancy K. Buckley and Hill M. Walker, pp. 53-68; *Living With Children: New Methods for Parents and Teachers* by Gerald R. Patterson and M. Elizabeth Gullion, pp. 37-42; *Teaching Social Behavior to Young Children* by William C. Sheppard *et al.,* pp. 41-58. Published by Research Press, 2612 N. Mattis, Champaign, Illinois 61820.

Analyzing Performance Problems by Robert F. Mager, pp. 7-15 and 51-89. Published by Fearon Publishers, 6 Davis Drive, Belmont, California 94002.

6
Using Social Reinforcers

The previous units have outlined the basic principles of social learning theory and have described a method for gathering data and for sharpening your observations of how you influence behavior. You should now be prepared to rearrange the learning environment in your school—

—to promote helpful and productive change among students, staff and parents
—to intervene effectively in the reinforcement process as it is played out daily in your classes
—to avoid potential difficulties in all phases of the school program: discipline, curriculum development, evaluation, and staff relations.

Social reinforcers are an inherent ingredient in teacher-student interaction. You, and students, already use them. Any verbal or non-verbal response by one person which influences the behavior of another person is a social reinforcer. For many people they are the strongest type of reinforcement, and they are certainly the most readily available, so they should be the first type of reinforcement that you use.

For most of your students, you are the most important reinforcing agent outside of their families or peer groups.

Your verbal and non-verbal responses will have a profound impact on your students—on their behavior patterns, on how they communicate, and even how they view school and their chance to succeed in life. Since we know how important social reinforcement is, it follows that teachers have a special responsibility to be careful, consistent, and aware of what behaviors they want to strengthen and what behaviors they want to weaken.

This is an ongoing responsibility—social reinforcement will occur every day whether you intend it or not. The question is whether you will be using it to advance each student's educational performance. If teachers are persistent and consistent in their reinforcing activities, the positive results should be readily apparent and should be a constant source of gratification.

It might be helpful to list some typical examples of social reinforcement commonly used in school.

VERBAL REINFORCERS

1. Teacher comments which are received as praise by students. The comments may be single words ("great," "excellent") or sentences ("I really like the way you're working today, John"). Both written and oral statements are involved here.

2. Engaging in a conversation which is enjoyable to a student, especially about his personal experiences and interests.

3. Acknowledging a student's entry into a room or his passing in the hall or street. A special signal may even have a more personal meaning here.

4. Offering to help a student in a pleasant tone of voice.

5. Calling on students in class by using descriptive phrases ("John really looks like he knows this answer").

6. Using your students' names in fun stories you present to the class.

7. Sending home to parents regular letters for good class performance (which is a written social reinforcement from the teacher), possibly asking parents to react with additional social reinforcement.

NON-VERBAL REINFORCERS

1. Holding eye contact with a student when he is seeking it.

2. Using a handshake or handslap as a greeting or acknowledgement of good performance.

3. Hugging, holding a student's arm lightly or bending your arm lightly around the student's neck when you have something special to say to him.

4. Standing close and maintaining proximity with students during class activities.

5. Esoteric signals between teacher and individual students or the whole group to signify some favorable outcome.

6. General facial expressions which are non-threatening and are even exaggeratedly open and inviting.

HOW DO YOU PRESENTLY USE
SOCIAL REINFORCEMENT?

You must analyze your present environment before attempting any major changes in discipline or curriculum.

1. Do you know how to make *each* of your students "beam" as a result of a verbal or non-verbal response from you? What typical phrases or terms do you usually use to express praise?

   Do the students seem to perceive these as pleasant and desirable?

   What phrases might you add?

2. Which common behaviors, if any, have you merely expected your students to perform without any reinforcement?

Is it worth directing social reinforcement to those behaviors to strengthen them?

3. Which five student behaviors do you most commonly praise?

Do the same students tend to receive the bulk of your praises? If so, who are they?

4. Which students tend to receive the least of your praises? Why?

What do students do that prevent them from receiving praise?

How can you arrange things differently so that they qualify for praise?

5. Do students who cause disruptions tend to seize more of your attention (even if you intend that attention to be unpleasant) than students who do not cause disruption? If so, who are they and what do they do that is most chronic?

6. Which three non-verbal gestures (involving face, hands, body) do you use most commonly to convey recognition, affection and satisfaction?

    What additional gestures might be useful?

7. Are there particular students who seem to need more social attention than you are now giving? If so, who are they?

8. Do you tend to rely on warnings or threats as a major discipline device? If so, what are your most typical phrases?

Which students do you warn the most?

9. Do you have to repeat statements and directions too often? If so, what is usually happening when you make your initial statements?

What should be happening?

10. Do you usually stand, sit near, or share eye contact with the same small group of students in your classes? If so, how can you gain closer proximity to more students?

11. Do you expect students to raise their hands as a signal for contributing to discussion or for asking questions? If so, do you find that many students do not bother to raise their hands and that you still respond to them when they yell out comments or questions?

Does this cause disorder?

What steps can you take to avoid disorderly discussion and constant yelling out?

Consideration of the above questions will help you analyze how you are currently employing social reinforcement in your classroom. The following are strategies for using social reinforcement to produce a specific change.

TO STRENGTHEN A DESIRED BEHAVIOR

—follow it as soon as possible with a verbal or non-verbal response that is pleasant to the student. The desired behavior may not be performed perfectly the first time so remember to reinforce steps *toward* the desired goal: reinforce each successive approximation. The social reinforcer must be given at the *appropriate time:* as soon as possible after the behavior occurs and before other intervening behaviors. Otherwise the potency of the reinforcement effort will be lessened. The reinforcement must be given for the *appropriate behavior:* do not give the same reinforcement for contradictory behaviors. The reinforcement must be given in the *appropriate form:* it must be perceived as pleasant by the recipient, so avoid embarrassing the student.

You may have to practice being socially reinforcing, adopting new behaviors of your own to turn your students on. With some children, you may have to search for opportunities to find a hint of good behavior—but when you find it, reinforce it. Be careful not to satiate students with exces-

also will inevitably end up arguing with a student over whether he knew that he was not to engage in some behavior because he did not hear the instructions. If possible, institute a rule that when there is too much noise, you will simply stop and raise your hand and will not proceed until there is quiet. Your attention, and where you choose to focus it, is the most potent factor in the classroom.

4.   Do not try to settle disputes by having children tell how it started until both students are removed from the situation. After removal, tell each they can tell their story once, and will not be allowed to interrupt the other. Then make your decision. For chronic fights between the same students, time out can be effective (but do not put both children behind the screen at the same time).

7

Using Non-Social Reinforcers

The previous unit described ways of organizing social reinforcers—verbal and non-verbal interpersonal communication. But there are several other types of reinforcing agents present in most school environments: (1) privileges and special activities, (2) material objects, (3) tokens, (4) grades and commendations and (5) edibles.

The selection of the most appropriate reinforcer is often a difficult choice. As a general rule, one should use social reinforcers for reasons detailed in the previous unit. But if they prove ineffective in dealing with the behavior you are trying to change, then you should consider other types of reinforcers.

Even if you are not intending to engage in a planned behavior change, you must be aware of the impact these other reinforcers have on the students in your classroom. If you use grades and various types of activities and privileges, then you are already distributing non-social reinforcers on a daily basis.

To the degree that you use reinforcers, planned or not, you should make sure they are employed in the most humane and thoughtful manner.

PRIVILEGES AND SPECIAL ACTIVITIES

These may include:
- —special jobs assigned to students such as roll taker or media operator
- —extra recess or breaks
- —talk time
- —favorite game time
- —access to special learning stations
- —informal group discussions on favorite topics such as cars, ghosts or television shows
- —free reading time
- —arts and crafts periods for mini-courses, macrame, kite making, model building, etc.
- —singing, dancing and playing fun music
- —parties
- —field trips

This category of reinforcer provides the most fertile possibilities for the typical school environment because the privileges are already there and it is simply a question of how to use them. If privileges and special activities are "given away" then you will have no control over how they influence and change your students' behavior. But there are several rules you can follow to help you remain in charge.

1. Make sure the privileges and special activities are made contingent upon performance of desired behavior.

2. Specify well in advance how they are to be earned. Do not throw them out as bait when things get out of hand. This smacks of bribery and also teaches the students that if they cause trouble, you will cough up a reward to make them stop. Privileges can strengthen bad behavior, so make sure they are earned only for good behavior.

3. Do not give these reinforcers on a group basis if you can avoid it. If students are made dependent upon other

members' behavior, they may become frustrated by others' non-compliance and begin not to respond to the opportunity to earn a privilege. More important, the rebels may be stimulated by their perception that they are "controlling" the system and may persist.

MATERIAL OBJECTS

These may include:
- —all types of regular and fun school supplies such as colored felt-tip pens
- —games and puzzles
- —records
- —posters
- —sports equipment
- —padlocks and bike locks
- —other material objects which the particular social environment of the students makes highly desirable (for example, "fuzzy feet" patches for clothes)

These should be used as a last resort because they may not be necessary; some teachers or parents may not like the notion of material reward; and they may present a budget problem. Most students are satisfied with school-related items, so expensive non-educational items can usually be avoided.

If your school has a store which sells supplies perhaps the store can be decentralized and supplies distributed to various classes for purchase with tokens earned in that class. The material items might have a set price to be paid in tokens, or they might be auctioned to the highest bidder (which can be fun, educational, and will let the students tell you how much the "price" ought to be).

Note: Students should not be required to earn material objects which are integral to their education and which they could not otherwise obtain.

TOKENS

Tokens are any tangible object or symbol which can be exchanged for a desired material reward, activity or privilege. They include such things as:
   —points
   —plastic chips
   —stars
   —special cards
   —play money

Tokens are useful for several reasons: (1) every student in the class can be involved with tokens, whereas every student can hardly receive a single teacher's attention constantly; (2) reinforcement can be delivered immediately and consistently; (3) students can be involved in the administering of the system and can learn basic elements of banking and currency flow (they can keep a list of the points they earn and table leaders can add up the daily totals); (4) by varying the types of things for which tokens can be exchanged, students begin to save for bigger rewards, thus learning to delay gratification—a valuable lesson in itself.

GRADES

Grades and other graphic commendations include:
   —letter symbols
   —number systems
   —faces— ☺ or ☹
   —letters to parents praising their child's performance
   —certificates of achievement
   —ribbons and medals

Grades are effective reinforcers only if they are viewed by students as accessible. Students who do not believe they can attain a high grade, or performance commendation, are likely to give up and not respond to symbols of academic achievement. The classic dropout profile often shows this. Three practices may need to be changed to prevent this. First, the tasks confronting each student should not be insurmountable (refer to Unit 3). Start at the level of capability of each student. Second, the criteria for judging accomplishment should be related to each individual (if you grade on a group "curve," then students on the bottom will quickly realize there is no reason to try). Third, grades should recognize effort, not perfection. After a student begins to attempt academic work and begins to respond to grades, then the criteria can be related to increasing quality.

The use of a numerical grading system can serve the purpose of evaluating performance and can also be converted into tokens exchangeable for privileges, activities or material objects.

Sending notes home to parents praising a student's work can be an especially potent reinforcer. For most students who have performed poorly academically or have been behavior problems, most notes home to parents have brought trouble. A praising note serves the double purpose of giving the student a performance commendation and soliciting social reinforcement for the student from the parents.

EDIBLES

Some edibles are appropriate for school use. These include:
- —juices
- —milk
- —baked goods
- —sugarless gum
- —fruit

Some persons use candy, soft drinks, and Kool Aid. But in considering any edible, teachers must be concerned with the effect of sugar, artificial sweeteners, and artifical coloring on children's health. Recent evidence suggests that they may have an adverse impact on behavior as well as general health.

Edibles may spark parental objection, even though many parents often try to influence children's behavior with Cokes and candy.

As with any reinforcer, the first step is to analyze how such reinforcers are already being used in your classroom, or are being made available because of school activities. The second step is to decide how you want to influence the use of such reinforcers.

TO STRENGTHEN A DESIRED BEHAVIOR

—reinforce regularly and consistently in the initial stages of shaping a behavior. As the behavior becomes well established, begin to reinforce the behavior intermittently rather than every time. Then attempt to fade out the non-social reinforcer.

When distributing non-social reinforcers, include social praise whenever possible. Remember, you are using non-social reinforcers only because social reinforcement was not effective by itself. If you pair social reinforcement with the non-social, substantial research evidence indicates the former will gain in potency. This makes it much easier to fade out the non-social reinforcer and build the social reinforcement process.

TO WEAKEN AN UNDESIRED BEHAVIOR

—decide what you would rather have the student do which would be incompatible with the undesired behavior. Then weaken the undesired behavior while strengthening the desired alternative. Two main strategies are used: withholding the reward and withdrawing the reward.

For *withholding*, the idea is to extinguish the undesired behavior through non-reinforcement. The method for receiving the reward—engaging in the desired behavior—is specified in advance. The undesired behavior receives nothing and when the preferred alternative is performed it is rewarded.

This is useful where the undesired behavior is not excessively disruptive and can be ignored.

For *withdrawing*, the reward is taken away when the undesired behavior occurs and then is reinstated when the preferred alternative is performed. This is best done with tokens (for example, the desired behavior earns 5 points; the undesired behavior loses 5 points). Using tokens is preferable because if you try to physically take a material reward away when a student is misbehaving then you may just foment rebellion.

CONTINGENCY CONTRACTS

Wherever possible, students should be involved in decisions on changing behavior. An effective technique is a contingency contract—a written agreement which specifies your expectation of the student (an academic task or a desired behavior) and his expectation of you (the reinforcement). The contract makes clear that the reward will be made contingent upon the student's performance.

Many teachers have found this indispensible for reorganizing their curriculum and individualizing instruction. Instructional tasks are broken down into sequences on a daily basis. As a student completes them, he checks them off on his contract and selects an appropriate reward from a "menu" that has been jointly selected by students and teacher.

The same type of agreement can be made for chronic behavior problems. The student agrees to change a specific behavior and the teacher agrees to keep a check on performance. If performance criteria are met, then mutually agreed upon reinforcement occurs.

The following is a simple example of a contract to change a social behavior.

(Student's name) and (Teacher's name) agree to the following:

If (Student's name) performs the positive behavior(s) listed below, (Teacher's name) will provide the reinforcement listed below.

Positive behavior(s): (List in specific terms the behavior to be performed. Specify the time, place and frequency of performance required. State how and when observations and evaluations are to be made).

Reward: (State the reinforcement in precise terms. Specify the time, place. frequency, and quantity in which the reinforcement will be provided for satisfactory performance).

(Student's signature)   (Teacher's signature)

     (date)   (date)

A simple contract for academic behavior could use the following format:

I, (Student's name), agree to complete the following learning activities, according to the (stated performance criteria) to obtain the (reinforcement listed below):

Learning activities: (List the activity or sequence of activities to be performed).

Requirements: (List the performance criteria to be used, as for example, % correct. Also state the time period allowed).

Reward: (State the grade or other reinforcer provided upon satisfactory performance).

(Student's signature)	(Teacher's signature)
(date)	(date)

HOW DO YOU PRESENTLY USE NON-SOCIAL REINFORCEMENT?

1. Describe the ways you already are using:

    privileges and special activities:

    material objects:

    tokens:

    grades and commendations:

    edibles:

2.   In what ways do you make them contingent upon desired academic or social behavior?

Do they strengthen the behaviors you want strengthened? If not, why?

3.   Make a list of additional non-social rewards which are available to you and which might be useful and appropriate:

privileges and special activities:

material objects:

tokens:

grades and commendations:

edibles:

Describe the student behaviors which you think need to be reinforced this way and consider how you might arrange it.

4. How can you involve your students in contingency contracts so that they can help make decisions about changing their behavior?

A much fuller explanation of the contracting process, as well as many examples of types of behavior faced by teachers can be found in: *How to Use Contingency Contracting in the Classroom* by Lloyd Homme *et al.; Writing Behavioral Contracts: A Case-Simulation Practice Manual* by William J. DeRisi and George Butz. Published by Research Press, 2612 N. Mattis, Champaign, Illinois 61820.

How Did It Work?

After attempting behavior change, if results are not satisfactory the following checklist should be used to find the trouble.

PROBLEM ANALYSIS

Did you focus on only one behavior at a time?

Did you describe the behavior in observable terms?

Did you record the frequency of the behavior?

Did you observe what you did following the behavior?

Did you communicate the discrepancy (between expected performance and actual behavior) to the student?

Did the student have a chance to succeed at the task?

Was there a positive consequence for performance?

Was there some punishment or other obstacle to performance?

Was non-performance rewarded?

Did you need to model the behavior to get it started?

Did you need to start with smaller pieces of the behavior and build successive approximations?

CHANGE STRATEGY

Did you try to increase performance of the desired behavior by positive reinforcement?

If so, did you make sure the reward was always perceived as pleasant?

Did you try to increase performance of the desired behavior by removing something unpleasant?

Did you try to decrease the undesired behavior by ignoring it and reinforcing an incompatible alternative?

EVALUATION

Did your reinforcement get static so that you needed to decrease the frequency of reinforcement and begin reinforcing only intermittently?

Did you pair social reinforcers with non-social reinforcers so that you could fade the non-social reinforcers out completely?

Appendix

Critical Issues for Discussion

THEORY

Is behavior regularly modified through everyday human inter-actions and communications, whether or not the participants intend to deliberately shape and maintain certain responses?

Is the reinforcement process an inescapable condition of human relationships?

How does this view of humankind contradict the notions embodied in psychoanalytic theory or self-actualization theories?

Is all behavior the product of the reinforcement process?

Does this theory seem to relate to your common experience as a human being?

PRACTICE

Are reinforcement techniques practical enough to be applied directly and consistently to the classroom?

Are reinforcement techniques so "mechanistic" that they demean the teachers and students involved?

Can enough relevant reinforcers be found in the school environment, particularly for older students, to make their systematic application effective?

ETHICS

Should behavior be intentionally modified in the schools?

Should people deny that they are modifying behavior (including their own) just because it is done unintentionally?

Are behavior modification techniques necessarily "oppressive" and "dehumanizing" devices aimed at enforcing conformity and docility?

Are there really any teaching techniques which cannot be misused and misdirected?

Can the reinforcement process be harnessed to develop personal freedom—self-control, creativity, individuality and independence?

Should teachers consider it a primary responsibility to make sure that the reinforcers in the school environment, which will be having an impact whether or not they are used by design, are systematically and humanely employed?

Is the use of extrinsic reinforcement in the schools merely a form of bribery?

Are grades, awards and teacher praise extrinsic reinforcers?

Should students be rewarded through extrinsic means for attempting to achieve?

Do all persons conduct all their daily tasks because they are operating under their own intrinsic reinforcement, or, do we all need other types of "pay-offs" for certain jobs?

If students do not appear to be intrinsically motivated, how far should we go with extrinsic rewards to help them?

What safeguards should be built into the use of negative reinforcers (such as "time out") to ensure that they are not abused?

Does the use of non-social reinforcement in the schools necessarily produce greed and materialism?

Who should decide what goals are proper, appropriate and desirable in changing behavior?

Who really decides now what behaviors should be legitimately changed?

How can we avoid the selection of the wrong goals?

How do we know which goals are right?

INNER STATES

Does all this concern for observable behavior seem to deny or ignore the existence of human "feelings"?

How do we know an individual is experiencing a feeling if we do not observe certain patterns of behavior (crying, laughing, verbal expressions, etc.)?

Are feelings subject to the same reinforcement process as other human responses?

By changing troublesome behavior, do we only "treat" the symptom of the underlying problem?

What underlies human behavior?

Are such concepts as "ego" and "self-actualization" anything more than intellectual constructs?

Should we base our educational techniques and goals on the inferences we make about why people function as they do?

Does working with one or a few behaviors at a time seem to ignore the "whole child"?

What does the term "whole child" mean beyond the behavior a child exhibits?

What does "learning" mean if it does not refer to the change of behavior through reinforced practice?

Notes